DODD, MEAD WONDERS BOOKS include WONDERS OF:

WONDERS OF
TIGERS

Sigmund A. Lavine

*Illustrated with photographs,
drawings, and old prints*

Fields Corner

DODD, MEAD & COMPANY
New York

For Garry—
a tiger among bulls and bears

Frontispiece: Siberian tiger

Illustrations courtesy of: Author's collection, 11 (top), 21, 30, 50, 58; Author's collection, photo by Nicholas J. Krach, 11 (bottom), 17, 18, 19, 46, 69, 73, 74; British Museum, 22; Cincinnati Bengals, 20 (right); Allan Daniels, 15; Detroit Tigers, 20 (left); Government of India, 36; Hirshhorn Museum and Sculpture Garden, Smithsonian Institution, Gift of Joseph H. Hirshhorn, 1966, 25; Mike Kops, 40-41; Photograph by Nicholas J. Krach, 38, 51, 67; Ted Lewin, 43, 54, 57; Library of Congress, 71; Alan S. Maltz, 34; Letitia Maye, 8, 12, 33, 75; New York Zoological Society Photo, 2, 6, 48, 61, 64; Jane O'Regan, 11 (center), 29, 37, 53; Elizabeth Philbrick, copyright Anne Philbrick Hall, 31; Smithsonian Institution, 39; © Smithsonian Institution, 1986, courtesy of the Freer Gallery of Art, 23.

Library of Congress Cataloging-in-Publication Data

Lavine, Sigmund A.
  Wonders of tigers.

  Includes index.
  Summary: Examines the life and lore of the tiger, including its physical characteristics, behavior, natural habitat, and relationship with man.
  1. Tigers—Juvenile literature. [1. Tigers] I. Title.
QL737.C23L37 1987   599.74'428   87-15721
ISBN 0-396-09153-9

CONTENTS

A Siberian tiger

1.
MEET THE TIGER

"All beasts of prey are strong
or treacherous."
—HERBERT

Tigers, along with other members of the cat family (Felidae), have a long history. Their first-known ancestors appeared during the Eocene epoch, some fifty million years ago. These creatures, like their modern descendants, were carnivores (meat eaters) and, as the centuries passed, they became skilled predators.

However, all forms of felids did not survive the shifts in climate and the geological upheavals that occurred from time to time. Nevertheless, paleontologists (experts in the dating and identification of fossils) have determined that the true cats were commonplace in the Pliocene epoch, which began about twelve million years ago. Still another two million years were to pass before the immediate progenitor of the tiger walked the Earth.

Contrary to widespread belief, the tiger's direct ancestor was not one of the several species of so-called saber-toothed tigers that once roamed the Old and New worlds, killing

A Bengal or Indian tiger. No two tigers have the same arrangement of stripes.

mammoths with their dagger-like teeth. In fact, the relationship between the saber-toothed cats and the present-day tiger is remote. Saber-toothed tigers belong to a group of animals that branched off from the other Felidae forty million years ago during the Oligocene epoch.

As the tiger evolved, other felids also were assuming their current forms. Eventually, the thirty-five species of existing cats developed. Science divides these into two groups: the great cats *(Panthera)* and the small cats *(Felis)*. While there are numerous technical differences between the two classifications, the main distinction is that the big cats—cheetah, clouded leopard, jaguar, leopard, lion, snow leopard, and tiger—roar but cannot purr while the small cats purr but cannot roar. Big cats are able to roar because they have a pliable cartilage at the base of the tongue. Instead of this cartilage, small cats have a bone.

It is generally accepted by wildlife experts that the modern tiger originated in Siberia. This belief is based on the discovery of the earliest known fossil remains of the true tiger in the Chigar Caves on the New Siberian Islands, well above the Arctic Circle. Similar finds have been dug up in the Lena River Valley in Russia and near the city of Harbin in central Manchuria.

Fossils also reveal that the first tigers spread over northern Asia and prospered. But, with the coming of the Ice Ages, they were forced to seek a more suitable habitat. A few tigers—their descendants are probably the closest to the original stock—remained in the northland despite the bitter cold, but most of the population trekked south until tropical or subtropical regions were reached.

This migration resulted in the distribution of the tiger over a vast area extending from easternmost Turkey through central Asia, the Indian subcontinent, Burma, and the islands of Bali and Java. There also were tigers in much of eastern China, North Korea, Manchuria, Afghanistan, and Iran.

Not only did the tiger once occupy a widespread range but also it was numerous throughout much of its habitat. Today, only a few thousand tigers live in the wild. They are spread thinly across Asia from Siberia to northern China and southward to the Malay Peninsula.

For years scientists were unable to agree on the number of subspecies of tiger or on their proper names. Finally, in 1979, Vratislav Mazak of Czechoslovakia, a world-famous authority on the tiger, revised the list of subspecies and their names. Mazak, whose revision is considered definitive, includes eight subspecies of tiger:

COMMON NAME	SCIENTIFIC NAME	RANGE
Bali tiger	*Panthera tigris balica*	Island of Bali
Caspian tiger	*Panthera tigris virgata*	From the Caspian Sea eastward to Afghanistan and northward to Russia
Chinese tiger	*Panthera tigris amoyensis*	South China
Indian tiger	*Panthera tigris tigris*	Most of India, Nepal, Bhutan, and western Burma, where its range overlaps that of *corbetti*
Indo-Chinese tiger	*Panthera tigris corbetti*	Southern China and eastern Burma to Vietnam and the Malay Peninsula
Javan tiger	*Panthera tigris sondaica*	Confined to Java
Siberian tiger	*Panthera tigris altaica*	Ussurian region of the Soviet Far East
Sumatran tiger	*Panthera tigris sumatrae*	Island of Sumatra

The Bali tiger, which may have been introduced into that island by man, is extinct, the last-known specimen having been shot in 1937. While it is barely possible that a few Caspian tigers still inhabit remote areas, the lack of sightings indicates that *virgata* is almost certainly extinct.

Meanwhile, it well may be that in a few years the only living tigers will be those exhibited in zoos or protected in national parks. Yet *tigris* can adapt to extremes of heat and cold and thrive in jungles, stands of coniferous trees, swamplands, rain forests, or mountainous terrains. All tigers demand

This Sumatran or tree tiger appeared in a zoology text nearly 200 years ago. It is likely that the artist never saw a Sumatran tiger, because the dashes and spots on the legs, the blotches on the flanks, and the broken rings on the tail resemble the markings of the clouded leopard more than those of the tree tiger. Sumatrae is not only darker than other tigers but also more heavily striped.

A Chinese tiger

Old print shows Javan tiger in a bold daytime attack on men traveling an isolated road. Today there are no man-eaters on that island. The Javan species is extinct.

Taken from the back of an elephant in India's Banhavgarh National Park, this photo makes it clear how the tiger blends into its habitat.

of a habitat is that it provide vegetation in which to hide and raise young, plenty of water, and an ample supply of prey.

Because there are many locales that meet these requirements, it would appear that the tiger's future should be assured. But, unfortunately, these areas also can furnish some of the lumber or farmland needed to house and feed the world's ever increasing population. Unless man uses bulldozer and chainsaw more wisely than he has in the past, free-roaming tigers may vanish from the Earth.

12

2.
LORE OF THE TIGER

"That's another story."
—TERRANCE

For untold centuries, the tiger has stimulated man's imagination. No one knows when *tigris* was first endowed with supernatural powers, but it must have been at a very early date. Thousands of years ago, the Chinese believed that a tiger stood at each of the four cardinal points of the compass and prevented horrible demons from entering the Earth. The South was secured by the red tiger of summer, the North defended by the black tiger of winter, the East watched over by the blue tiger of vegetation, and the West guarded by the white tiger of autumn. Legend held that these four tigers were responsible to their brother, a huge yellow tiger that lived in the center of the Earth, which the Chinese thought was directly beneath their country.

Not only did the Chinese maintain that tigers protected them but also they endowed *tigris* with the ability to bestow great wealth upon an individual, ward off his enemies, and keep him well. Thus it was formerly the custom to attempt

13

to flatter the tiger by embroidering its likeness on one's clothes. Military men, convinced that *tigris* favored brave warriors, ordered that tigers be painted on the weapons of their troops.

In ancient times, even the wisest of men were convinced that all tigers were female and the father of all tiger cubs was the West Wind! Many of the current superstitions about *tigris* are just as fantastic. Malayan folklore holds that tigers live in a city of houses built of human bones and thatched with human hair. This city is said to be ruled by a wise but wicked old tiger.

Generally speaking, superstition links *tigris* with evil. Primitive peoples firmly believe that sorcerers employ tigers to help them work black magic. The Chams of southern India say witches and wizards ride tigers during their diabolical nocturnal activities. Certain tribesmen hold that witches can turn humans into tigers. However, there is no difficulty in distinguishing these animals—they have no tails!

Throughout Asia, it is widely held that tigers bent on mischief have the ability to assume human form. Tribal taletellers recount yarns describing how tigers transform themselves into beautiful maidens, marry unsuspecting hunters, and then bring misfortune or death to their husbands. In Korea, tigers intending to harm humans are thought to change themselves into wise old monks. It is not difficult for a tiger to make this transformation. All it has to do is somersault forward three times. To regain its natural form, *tigris* need only make three backward somersaults.

Perhaps the most widely distributed superstition featuring *tigris* is the contention that man-eating tigers enslave the ghosts of the humans they kill. The only way such a ghost can gain its freedom is to bring its master another human

The tiger, long considered a malevolent, bloodthirsty beast, has been linked with evil by the superstitious.

victim. Until this is done, the ghost is forced to attack cattle and destroy crops.

Although these ghosts are greatly feared, they are not held responsible for as much damage as the invisible tigers the credulous believe are sent by gods to punish men. Even more malicious—so it is said—are the tigers that carry out the commands of sorcerers.

Out of their fear of these phantom tigers, jungle-dwelling tribes have developed curious customs. Among them is the saving of the first hair cut from a child's head. Superstition decrees that if this is not done, the youngster's father will be eaten by a ghost tiger.

Some tribes maintaining that *tigris* is very sensitive and easily insulted engage in rites to appease it. Country folk in Sumatra hesitate to use a tiger's trail for fear the animal will resent their trespassing. Nor do they look behind them when walking at night—to do so might offend any tiger prowling nearby.

Amulets fashioned from tiger claws, teeth, and whiskers are thought to have wondrous powers. These charms are worn in Asia to insure the affections of a loved one, bring good fortune, and, as well as making their owners extremely brave and daring, provide protection from demons, evil men, and sudden fright. However, if a tiger's whisker is ritually cursed by a practitioner of black magic and secretly fastened to a rival's clothing, it will bring about that rival's downfall.

So great was the fear of the magic of the tiger that native trappers and hunters in earlier times apologized for snaring and killing the great beast. Indeed, it was the custom of the Bataks of India, who destroyed only man-eating tigers, to ask their gods to explain to the tigers why it was necessary to kill them.

These attempts to appease a dead tiger's spirit may not have stemmed solely from fear. They may have grown out of the conviction that tigers were originally humans—a transmutation that is prominent in Far Eastern mythology. A tale from Nepal tells of a man and woman who were turned into tigers after escaping from a flood, while Malayan lore contends that the first tiger was a lazy schoolboy who fled into the jungle. Such legends imply that *tigris* and man are kin. Thus it is understandable that hunters ask forgiveness

16

Henry O. Forbes, famous English naturalist and explorer, drew this sketch of a tiger trap while studying wildlife in Sumatra between 1878 and 1883.

for killing a tiger and why tiger flesh is taboo in some societies. On the other hand, there are those who claim tiger meat makes one as fierce and strong as the animal from which it comes. But, in the Miris tribe of India, only the men are allowed to eat tiger. The meat is forbidden to women because it might make them too strong minded!

Tiger worship is commonplace from the icy forests of Siberia to the steaming jungles of the Malay Archipelago. Manchurian tribes pay homage to effigies of tigers fastened to the tops of tall poles. In India, elaborate ceremonies are held honoring the tiger gods Bagheswar and Kinnasoms. *Tigris* is also important in the religion of the Saki and other forest-dwelling tribes of the Malay Peninsula.

17

In addition to being worshiped, *tigris* is associated with various divinities. Tibetans hold that Da, the deity credited with helping men overcome their enemies, bears a tiger on his right shoulder as he rides across the heavens. Tao-ling, founder of modern Taoism, an Oriental religion, is always pictured riding a tiger. Despite the fact that Hindu mythology maintains tigers are punished after death for their evil ways, *tigris* is a close companion of several Hindu gods, including Siva, one of the three supreme Hindu deities. Siva's consort, Parvarti, is also linked with *tigris*. 'Tis said she rides a tiger as she travels about protecting the deserving from misfortune. Hindu tradition also states that the great goddess Katyayati rides in a chariot drawn by a tiger. Many Oriental representations of the zodiac depict Buddha, the great religious leader, being drawn across the sky in a cart harnessed to a tiger.

Juvenal, the satirical Roman poet, described a general as being "as fierce as a tiger plundered of her cubs." This simile makes an obvious comparison. So does the Chinese "He is a

Legend links numerous Oriental deities with tigris. *The tiger is also thought to be the companion of wise men throughout the Far East. Thus Tao-ling, founder of modern Taoism, is always pictured riding a tiger.*

18

This picture of "Young Tigers at Play with a Dog" illustrated a children's book over a hundred years ago. The author advised his readers that "the Tiger, when captured very young, is quite tameable but it is always a dangerous pet."

paper tiger" and the Telegu "At home a tiger, abroad a spider." But the meaning of the Malayan "He sits like a tiger withdrawing its claws" is, like that of many similes featuring the tiger, obscure. It likens an individual gloating over a rival's downfall to a tiger that has just made a kill.

Many proverbs concerning *tigris* also require explanation. The Korean saying "A day old puppy fears not the tiger" implies that those who do not recognize danger are never afraid. To warn an individual that he should be prepared for every contingency, the Marathi of India advise, "When hunting the hare, take weapons used in hunting the tiger."

But there is nothing subtle about the Indian proverb, "Where deer are plentiful, there is no tiger." Equally clear in meaning are the Javanese "If you back a monkey, he will fight a tiger" and "When the tiger is dead, the deer dance on its grave."

Popular speech has not neglected the tiger. Professional wrestlers are called "tigermen," Detroit's American League baseball team is known as "the Tigers," and winners of sporting events are given "Three Cheers and a Tiger!" Meanwhile, the slang term "tiger" has a different meaning in the United States from the one it has in England. Englishmen use it as an insult applied to individuals who lack manners. Americans employ the word as a good-natured jibe at lively young men.

Georges Clemenceau, who guided France during World War I, and other statesmen noted for their tenacity and fighting spirit have been nicknamed "the Tiger." This label has also been applied to the athletic teams of many schools, including Depauw, Louisiana State, and Princeton universities.

Official logo of the Detroit Tigers baseball club and a tiger-striped helmet of the Cincinnati Bengals football team.

Thomas Nast drew this picture of the Tammany Tiger.

Undoubtedly the most famous group to bear the name of *tigris* was composed of the daring aviators of World War II who, under the command of General Claire Chennault, flew over the towering Himalayas to bring desperately needed supplies to General Joseph (Vinegar Joe) Stilwell while his forces drove the Japanese invaders out of Burma. These aviators called themselves "The Flying Tigers."

When Thomas Nast, the famous cartoonist, chose the tiger as the symbol of Tammany, the dishonest political organization that controlled New York City in the late nineteenth century, he was not being original. *Tigris* has stood for greed, intrigue, power, and stealth for centuries. The tiger also represents bloodthirstiness, cruelty, and savagery.

21

No depiction of tigris *is more finely detailed than "Tiger by a Torrent," painted by the outstanding Japanese artist Nishi Ganka in 1795. Ganka portrayed his subject in ink and colors on a hanging silk scroll.*

But the tiger also serves to typify favorable characteristics. In Korea, where *tigris* is considered the King of Beasts, the tiger personifies both physical beauty and military force. In China, a white tiger is symbolic of longevity. Europeans consider it a great honor to have a tiger in their coat of arms. This indicates that one's family has displayed great valor on the battlefield and, further, that it is extemely dangerous to arouse that family's members.

Tigris also serves as a symbol in Oriental painting. When the Japanese artists of yesteryear wished to picture evil, they placed a tiger in a bamboo grove. In addition, both Chinese

22

and Japanese masters of the brush have long depicted tigers engaged in various activities. Usually these pictures are painted on hanging silk scrolls with both ink and colors. Typical of these exquisite creations is Nishi Ganka's "Tiger by a Torrent."

Ganka's work has been recorded along with those of other early artists, but the names of many who portrayed *tigris* on scroll and rice paper are lost. An unknown craftsman painted the lifelike tiger stalking across the fresco that brightens the walls of an ancient burial chamber in Gukenri, Korea. He, as well as the majority of ancient workers in metal and stone who fashioned tigers in China during the Chang and Chous dynasties, is forgotten, but the creations of all still continue to delight the mind and eye.

The wondrously executed tigers of Chinese and Japanese artists are rivaled by those produced from 1526 to 1765 by painters at the courts of the Mogul emperors of India. It was the duty of such artists to record the activities of their masters. As the emperors spent much of their time hunting—

The name of the metalworker who fashioned this bronze tiger in China during the ninth century B.C. is unknown. However, it has been established that the bronze was used as a sacrificial vessel.

they were the only ones allowed to kill tigers—court painters often pictured them battling ferocious beasts.

Today, *tigris* is still a favorite subject of Far Eastern artists. Modern depictions of the tiger range from those rivaling in beauty and technique pictures painted centuries ago to pencil drawings, oils, and watercolors designed to appeal to tourists.

Nor has the tiger been neglected in European art. Antoine Louis Barye, a famous French engraver, painter, and sculptor, was so captivated by the lithe beauty of *tigris* that he not only modeled statues of tigers but also painted the spectacular "Tiger Searching for Prey" that hangs in the Louvre. Paris' fabulous museum also holds two other such renowned paintings: Eugene Delacroix's "Young Tiger with Its Mother" and "Horse Attacked by Tiger." A lithograph by Edvard Munch of the tiger he watched for hours in the zoo in Copenhagen, Denmark, is another magnificent portrayal of *tigris*.

Like the artists of times past, contemporary etchers, engravers, painters, photographers, and sculptors find *tigris* a fascinating subject. Meanwhile, the manufacturers of fine porcelains, along with makers of inexpensive pottery, produce representations of the tiger. Large and small tigers also are fashioned from cloth, glass, metal, and wood by craftsmen and machines throughout the world.

Although roustabouts sang of "going to see the devil and a tiger fight" as they loaded freight on the paddle-wheelers that once steamed up and down the Mississippi River, composers have taken little note of *tigris*. However, the tiger stalks through a vast jungle of literature. From ancient times to the present, the tiger has inspired writers.

Among the Roman authors who mention *tigris* are the

Antoine Louis Barye, famous French engraver, painter, and sculptor, was fascinated with the tiger's lithe beauty. "Tiger Devouring an Antelope" (c.1830) is one of his most famous statues of tigris.

naturalist Pliny the Elder and the historian Suetonius. While their descriptions of the animal and its habits were inaccurate, they were not as farfetched as those set down by two learned Greeks. One of these was Ktesian, noted for telling "amazing lies about scenes he had not witnessed and knew his readers had not." The other was Aristotle, whose writings influenced the thinking of educated men well into the Middle Ages. According to Aristotle, a tiger had: "A triple set of teeth in both the upper and lower jaw....a sting in its tail and...the facility of shooting-off the spines that are attached to its tail."

It is doubtful that an individual who had never seen a tiger would recognize one from Aristotle's report. But the account of "brightly striped lions" set down by Marco Polo in the thirteenth century upon his return from China would, very likely, help in the identification of *tigris*.

The monks of medieval times included the tiger in their bestiaries, treatises ascribing moral traits to animals. Then, as the centuries passed, the tiger became prominent in all types of literature from Shakespeare to short stories. Incidentally, the most famous short story ever written about the tiger is Frank R. Stockton's "The Lady or the Tiger."

Poets in many lands have also sung of *tigris*. Modern versifiers that have done so include, among others, Joanne Baille, Hilaire Belloc, John Bennet, T.S. Eliot, Walter H. Kerr, Ruth Potter, and Sylvia T. Warner. But none of their poems convey as much mystic beauty as William Blake's "The Tiger," source of those famous lines:

Tiger! tiger! burning bright
In the forests of the night,...

Until recent years, most books about tigers were written by big game hunters. The majority of these volumes are forgotten. But in numerous modern books designed to delight young readers, a tiger is a main character. Perhaps the best-known fictional tigers are A.A. Milne's Tigger, who bounced into the Forest in *The House At Pooh Corner*, and Shere Khan, the tiger that dominates Kipling's *The Jungle Book*. Actually, a large menagerie of tigers can be captured in the writings of Lotta Cottswell, Roger L. Green, So-un Kim, Ethel Macfarland, Barbara Picard, Dorothy Shuttlesworth, Charlotte Zolotow, and others.

But long before modern writers were retelling fairy tales and creating both fierce and friendly tigers, tribal story tellers in Asia were spinning yarns about *tigris*. Many of these tales detail how the powerful tiger was outwitted by a

clever bird, deer, or mouse. Interestingly enough, although there are no wild tigers outside Asia, East African tribesmen relate how Anansi, the spider, hoodwinked the great cat. *Tigris* also appears in the folklore of Jamaica.

Professors debate how *tigris* secured a place in the folklore of East Africa and an island in the Caribbean Sea. But that dispute is minor compared to the one over the origin of a story told in the cabins of slaves before the War Between the States. It begins: "Long ago when lions, elephants, tigers, and all that kind of vermin lived on the banks of the Mississippi...."

3.
PHYSICAL CHARACTERISTICS

"Did you ever see the like?"
—SWIFT

At first glance, all tigers look alike because of their distinctive coloring. However, despite this strong family resemblance, there are differences between tigers found in one region and those native to another.

Certain dissimilarities displayed by the various subspecies are adaptions for survival in a particular habitat. For example, tigers living in the cold of the far north wear long, thick, pale-colored coats. Such pelage not only insulates them but also enables them to blend into their snow-covered surroundings when hunting prey. Tigers in the tropics, on the other hand, have short, dark fur that provides excellent camouflage in the tall grass and dense underbrush of the steaming jungle.

In addition to variations in the length and shading of their handsome striped coats, the subspecies differ in other ways. Attention is called to these differences in the pages that follow. Otherwise, it is to be understood that the physical feature described is common to all tigers.

Size

Modern naturalists make every effort to determine with accuracy the weight and length of the tigers they tranquilize during research in the wild and in zoos. But the figures set down in earlier days by explorers, hunters, and even some students of wildlife are open to question. This is because there are two ways of measuring a tiger's body—"between pegs" and "over curves."

When a tiger is measured "between pegs," one peg is placed at its nose, another at the tip of its tail. The animal is then moved out of the way and the distance between the two pegs recorded. No pegs are employed in the "over curves" method, in which the tiger is measured along its back, following the curves of the body. This technique adds from two to six inches to a specimen's length.

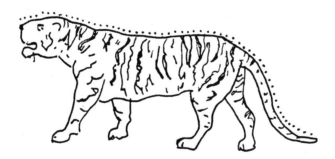

Sketch shows measuring a tiger by the "over curves" method, along the back from tip of nose to tip of tail.

The measuring of kills by "over curves" enabled many hunters to brag that they had shot extremely large tigers. Moreover, it was once the custom in India to measure tigers shot by visiting dignitaries with a special tape. The tape had only eleven inches to a foot!

This hybrid of a lion and a tigress is known as a "liger." Old print is of animal displayed in the Edinburgh Royal University Museum in the early 1800s.

Not only are Bengal and Siberian tigers the largest of the cats but also they rank among the largest felids that ever existed. On the other hand, Javan and Sumatran tigers, the smallest subspecies, are only about the size of a large leopard. Incidentally, although all tigers have narrower and slimmer bodies than lions, it takes an expert to distinguish between the skeletons of the two species.

Reports of Siberian tigers thirteen feet long and weighing seven hundred pounds are commonplace. However, the largest-known specimen "with reliable measurements" was an eleven-foot, six-inch male shot in Manchuria in 1943. Interestingly enough, the record for weight is held by another Siberian male. It tipped the scales at 845 pounds!

Bengal tigers do not attain the size of Siberian tigers. The record for this subspecies, commonly called the Indian tiger, is 558 pounds. Major James Corbett, the renowned hunter/author, is credited with shooting the largest known Bengal. Nicknamed the "Bachelor of Powalgarh," this infamous man-eater was ten feet, seven inches long.

Drawing on authenticated measurements made by the Maharajah of Cooch Behar of over six hundred Indian tigers and by current field studies, zoologists have determined that the average male Indian tiger is between eight and ten feet long, stands three feet high at the shoulder, and weighs from 400 to 450 pounds. The average female of this subspecies, like the females of all subspecies, is shorter and lighter.

It has been established also that Javan and Sumatran male tigers average between seven and eight feet from head to tail tip, measure twenty-nine inches at the shoulder, and weigh between 220 and 380 pounds. Measurements and weights of the remaining subspecies place them between the small island-dwelling tigers of Indonesia and the large tigers that inhabit the Asian mainland.

Irrespective of size, every tiger has a physique designed for creeping up on prey rather than running it down. Tigers may display sinuous grace when stalking, but their lithe, elongated bodies are packed with a maze of powerful

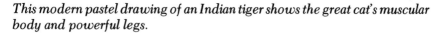

This modern pastel drawing of an Indian tiger shows the great cat's muscular body and powerful legs.

muscles that give them tremendous strength. Adult Indian tigers have no difficulty in dragging an animal weighing half a ton several hundred yards up a rocky hillside. It would take at least three men to duplicate this feat.

Coloration

All tigers have the same basic coloration: a ground color ranging from reddish-fawn to tawny-orange broken up by transverse bands. Usually the bands are black but they may be brown, gray, or grayish-brown. Cheeks. chest, muzzle, throat, underparts, whiskers, and the insides of the ears are white. The backs of the ears are black with conspicuous central white spots.

There is also a white area barred with black lines just above the eyes. These and similar lines on the side of the face form patterns comparable to human fingerprints—no two are the same. This makes it possible to identify individual tigers and to tell one animal from another.

Like facial markings, the stripes vary from one tiger to another. Stripes differ not only in color but also in width, length, and pattern. In many instances, the stripe pattern on one flank doesn't match that on the other. Moreover, the stripes of tigers in some areas are greatly reduced on the forelegs, shoulders, and rear of the flanks. In such cases, black spots appear between the normal black banding on back and flanks. They can be seen between the dark bars that transverse the background color.

Obviously, no book the size of this one can describe fully the numerous differences in coloration. Then, too, many of the dissimilarities are so minor that only zoologists specializing in the *Panthera* are concerned with them.

But the coloring of one group of tigers is of great interest to expert and nonexpert alike—the fabulous white tigers of

Note the pattern of stripes barring the coat of this Bengal tiger photographed in India. Not only does the space between the stripes vary but also the width and arrangement of the stripes differ on the legs, tail, and body.

India. These gorgeous creatures are not true albinos (animals with pure white fur and pink eyes). Although the ground color of these spectacular tigers is a creamy or eggshell white, they have black-brown stripes, ice-blue eyes, and pink noses.

White tigers are extremely rare in the wild. All captive specimens are descendants of a male caught some years ago

33

These white tigers were photographed at the Miami Metrozoo. One almost seems to be pulling the other out of the moat.

34

in the Rewa district of India. Hoping to raise white tigers, the ruler of Rewa mated the male with a normally pigmented female. None of her cubs were white. But when the male was bred to one of his daughters, that litter included young with their father's coloring. Today, white tigers are prized exhibits in a few zoos that have assumed the responsibility for perpetuating the strain.

Head

If a beauty contest were held for animals, the tiger would undoubtedly be a finalist. Not only does it have an eye-pleasing body but also it possesses a magnificent head, the attractiveness of which is enhanced by an alert expression and large eyes. A tiger's eye has a dark brown pupil surrounded by a yellow iris.

Like all felids, tigers have facial whiskers. Actually "feelers," these long, stiff, sensitive hairs permit cats to move about freely in the dark. No two tigers have the same arrangement of whiskers. As with facial markings, the pattern differs from one individual to another.

Besides whiskers, tigers have a beard-like growth of hair on the cheeks. It is more pronounced in males than in females and, in some individuals, it is larger or smaller, depending on the season. The "beard" is most developed in Sumatran tigers, which are also more apt than the other subspecies to have a short neck mane.

Because a tiger's skull is foreshortened, the leverage of the jaw is greatly increased. This, plus the strength of the massive muscles that control the jaw movement, enables tigers not only to hold prey in a viselike grip but also to pierce the toughest skin and sinew with their great teeth.

Tigers have thirty teeth in their tremendously powerful jaws, the lower of which can only be moved up and down.

Snarling tiger in Kanha National Park, Madhya Pradesh, India, displays its teeth.

Their slightly curved, well-rooted canines, or cutting teeth, are the largest of any land-dwelling carnivore. Moreover, the sharp tips and jagged edges of the last upper premolar and the first lower premolar—the so-called carnassial teeth—fit together perfectly, forming a pair of shears. To use the carnassials effectively, tigers have to compensate for the limited movement of the lower jaw. When feeding, they seize meat along the side of the mouth and then rip the flesh to pieces. Bones are ground with the upper carnassials, which are broad at the top. Bits of flesh are removed from bones with a tongue that, studded with pointed, recurved, hornlike projections called papillae, is used as a rasp.

Although their jaws, teeth, and tongue permit them to kill and butcher animals larger than themselves, tigers lack chewing teeth. Therefore, instead of chewing food before swallowing, tigers crush it.

Legs

Tigers walk on their toes. Only the naked, rubbery pads on the bottoms of their well-haired feet touch the ground. There are five toes on the foreleg paws, but the pollux (thumb) is placed well above the other toes and leaves no impression. The hind feet have four toes, the hallux (big toe) being absent.

Pug marks of male (left) and female (right) tigers of the same age.

Walking on their toes gives tigers a soft, noiseless tread that helps them get close enough to other animals so they can use their powerful legs effectively. The hind legs are longer than the front ones—an adaption that enables tigers to jump over obstacles and leap onto a quarry with battering-ram force. While the rear legs are brawny, the more heavily muscled forelimbs are even stronger. A blow struck with one of them can break the neck of a good-sized animal.

Not only are the legs crammed with muscles but also they are armed with strong three- to four-inch-long compressed claws. Except when being used to seize prey or for defense, the claws are retracted and sheathed in folds of skin. Otherwise, not only would they be blunted by constant contact with the ground but also they would make a noise whenever a tiger walked on a hard surface, thus alerting prospective prey. The claws are extended or withdrawn by a muscle and a tendon. When the muscle is contracted, the tendon pulls the last toe bones forward, causing the claws to emerge. When the muscle is relaxed, the claws retract.

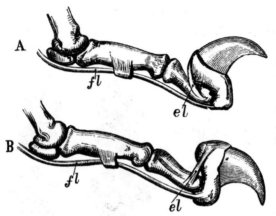

Tiger's foot: (A) Claw in ordinary position; (B) Claw unsheathed; (fl) Tendon of the muscle that extends the claw; (el) Elastic ligament that retracts the claw.

A tiger's normal gait is almost a glide, both limbs on the same side moving simultaneously. During a night's hunt, tigers cover from ten to twenty miles, walking at an average speed of about three miles an hour. When fleeing danger or attacking prey, tigers break into a gallop. While galloping, they increase their speed by bending the back and bringing the rear feet up in front of the forefeet. They may cover thirteen feet in a single bound. A.A. Dunbar Brander, an authority on the animals of Asia, reports seeing tigers in India leap across ditches twenty feet wide and clear fences six feet high. Zoologist Nikolai Baiko writes of a Siberian tiger whose springs averaged twenty feet on level ground and thirty-three feet during a downhill gallop. But the record for leaping must be awarded to a Bengal tiger. It jumped eighteen feet into the air to pull a man out of a tree!

Tail

Tigers' tails range from thirty inches to four feet in length. Those of most specimens are half the body length, but some tigers have tails that are nearly as long as their bodies. On

A tiger's body is packed with muscles that enable it to leap twenty feet or more over level ground, jump fifteen feet into the air, and kill animals twice its size. Note the extended claws and tail as this specimen jumps toward its prey.

the other hand, large tigers often bear tails that are very short in proportion to their size.

Like domestic cats, tigers use their tails as balancing poles when climbing and as rudders when jumping. The tail is also a means of communication, its position and motion indicating mood and intention.

Voice

Although tigers are relatively silent animals, they have a sizable vocal repertoire. It includes coughs, growls, grunts, hisses, howls, meows, moans, snarls, and roars of various kinds, along with other cries and calls.

With the exception of the plaintive meowing of cubs and the gentle puffing sound made as a friendly greeting, tigers' vocalizations are either ear-splitting or awesome. Of them all, none is so blood chilling as the *aa-oom* roared by an Indian tiger when announcing a kill, seeking a mate, or warning other tigers to leave the area unless prepared to

The sound of an Indian tiger's aa-oom, *employed when announcing a kill, seeking a mate, or warning other tigers away, is enough to chill the blood.*

fight. Resonant, the two-toned *aa-oom* reverbrates across the countryside, carrying for as much as two miles on a still night.

An excited or angry Indian tiger roars with increasing frequency and intensity. One tigress gave voice 266 times in an hour and a quarter!

Although females often roar to call their cubs if the youngsters are far away, they teach their offspring to follow them by uttering a soft grunt. This sound is in direct contrast to the variety of ferocious vocalizations tigers employ when about to attack a human, during a dispute with another tiger, or while fighting.

Tigers are noisiest during courtship, when they constantly groan, moan, and roar. None of these sounds is pleasing to the human ear. Indeed, one naturalist described the clamor caused by a tigress and two males vying for her affections as "a din like the caterwauling of midnight cats magnified a hundredfold."

Senses

Naturalists and hunters agree that tigers have keen senses of sight and hearing. However, they argue whether or not tigers have an acute sense of smell. This is nothing new. According to an ancient Burmese proverb, "If a tiger had to depend upon its nose, it would starve to death." In contrast, an early Sanskrit poem describes the tiger as "...an animal that has a highly developed sense of smell."

While the experts debate, a tiger employs its nose to pick up the scent of urine and feces left by other members of its subspecies at the boundaries of territories. By sniffing, tigers can tell not only how recently such a "mark" was left but also whether the territory is claimed by a male or a female. Moreover, by smelling a pug (footprint), a tiger can determine if it is an old impression or freshly made.

The nose also plays a part in courtship. The scent given off by females seeking mates draws suitors to them. Similarly, cubs unable to see their mother in tall grass have no difficulty trailing after her—they follow by smelling the ground where their parent has walked.

Thus it is obvious that the olfactory sense of tigers is very important in their relationships with one another. However, it is entirely possible that, unless visibility is limited, tigers do not depend to any great degree on their sense of smell while hunting.

As noted, tigers have excellent eyesight. Their large, bulging eyes are set on the sides of the head and directed forward. This gives them a wide field of vision. As a result, tigers accurately judge distances when stalking prey, although they do have difficulty in spotting motionless animals in the shade. But the slightest movement—a flick of the tail or a toss of the head—catches their notice.

Tigress photographed from a jeep in Ranthambhore National Park, India, rubs and sniffs tree after scent marking.

43

Actually, during daylight hours, tigers see only about as well as the average human. In poor light, their sight is approximately six times sharper than man's. This is because their eyes are quick to react to sudden darkness, the pupils dilating in order to admit the largest amount of whatever light there is. Conversely, in strong light, the pupils contract into ovals.

While the dilation of the pupils increases a tiger's vision in poor light, most of its ability to see in the dark is due to a special layer of cells called the "tapetum." This acts as a reflector, throwing back and brightening even the dimmest light received by the pupils.

Despite having night vision, tigers depend mainly on their hearing during nocturnal hunts. Employing their upright round ears as antennae, they twitch them back and forth in order to pinpoint the direction from which a sound is coming.

It has long been claimed that tigers "can even hear the breathing of a hunter in a hide." In all likelihood, this is true. Kalash Sankhala, a pioneer in the management of tiger reserves in India, offers proof that tigers actually can distinguish among the sounds made by the feet of various animals. In his book *Tiger!* Sankhala tells of a sleeping tiger that paid no attention when a mongoose scurried by and merely raised its head when a jackal passed. But with the first sound of rolling stones produced by a herd of deer, he immediately got up and fixed his eyes in that direction.

4.
WAYS OF THE TIGER

*"Most things are easy to learn
but hard to master."*
—CHINESE PROVERB

Until recently, most observations of the tiger were made through the sights of a rifle. A few of the trophy-seeking hunters of yesteryear, however, had an avid interest in the tiger's habits. But, unfortunately, instead of recording only what they saw, these individuals also accepted as fact everything their native guides told them. Therefore, their writings about *tigris* contain considerable misinformation. Then, too, the majority of hunters-turned-authors sought to justify their wholesale slaughter of tigers by labeling the animal a treacherous and bloodthirsty creature. Indeed, the writings of such men as J. Inglis, who hunted tigers in India and Nepal in the late 1880's, are responsible for the current widespread belief that the tiger "is the embodiment of devilish cruelty, of hate, and savagery incarnate."

Modern field studies have established that the tiger is not the vicious creature described by Inglis. But gathering accurate information about *tigris* has been a difficult task. This is

45

Nineteenth-century writers labeled the tiger a bloodthirsty animal full of hate. This is not true.

because numerous tigers do not conform to the normal behavior pattern of their subspecies. Perhaps nothing better illustrates the tendency of tigers "to do their own thing" than a report by Valmik Thapar, internationally famous authority on the Indian tiger. Thapar tells of a male tiger that did not stalk prey in the usual manner but instead charged into lakes to kill deer feeding on water plants.

Temperament

Tigris is frequently accused of being cowardly. This charge is false. Nevertheless, there is a reason for it's being made. Contact with humans has forced the tiger to be extremely cautious and take great pains to avoid being seen or drawing attention to itself. Intelligent animals, tigers have learned the advantages of being wary.

However, tigers can be bold and daring. Man-eating tigers, whose numbers are exceedingly small, have been known to snatch their victims out of carts moving along well-traveled roads. Tigresses know no fear when defending their cubs— few animal mothers are more protective of their young. Throughout Asia, audacious four-footed "rustlers" take a tremendous toll of livestock every year because they have learned that it is far easier to kill pastured goats than it is to run down a deer.

Except when courting or caring for young, tigers usually live alone, seeking seclusion and freedom from interference by others of their race. Tigers demand "personal space." Proof positive that tigers normally have little to do with one another—although all are aware of their neighbor's movements—was furnished by the radio-tracking conducted by the Smithsonian Tiger Ecology Project. During this study, radio transmitters were placed on nearly a thousand tranquilized tigers. Careful monitoring of the resulting signals indicated that only five percent came from sites where two tigers were fraternizing. Because of the field studies made by the Smithsonian and other institutions, as well as individuals, we know more about the life history and habits of the Indian tiger than of any other subspecies. Thus, the material that follows deals mainly with *Panthera tigris tigris*.

The Day of the Tiger

Although tigers are restless creatures, they spend much of their time relaxing or sleeping. Some tigers choose isolated shady nooks. Others prefer to lie up near a water hole where prey animals come to drink at dusk. Still others loll in the

A Siberian tiger cub takes a cooling drink.

open. But, as noted, even when *tigris* is dozing, it is aware of any activity in the immediate area and promptly awakes.

No matter where they rest, tigers get up and stretch now and then, or go to the nearest water for a drink. In hot weather, Indian tigers cool off by half-submerging themselves and soaking. But while *tigris* delights in bathing, it dislikes getting its face wet. Therefore, tigers always back into water, even when about to swim. Indian tigers are outstanding swimmers. In the Sundarbans, the vast area of swampland along India's Bay of Bengal, they swim considerable distances to get from one island to another, even in rough seas.

Hunting, not swimming, becomes more important to *tigris* as the shadows lengthen. But before seeking prey, a tiger uses its rough tongue as a washcloth and gives its paws and body their second grooming of the day—the first having taken place early in the morning. *Tigris* spends about half an hour washing. Then, after yawning a few times, the great cat goes looking for food. If it is lucky, the hunt will not last all night.

Hunting

Although called "the mighty predator," *tigris* often goes two or three days without making a kill. Indeed, no animal works harder for its food than the tiger. It succeeds in pulling down prey only once in every twenty attempts. Because a tiger cannot run at top speed for a long period, fleet-footed animals easily outdistance it. Slower creatures escape by dashing to rough ground or thorny areas. They are not pursued there because the pads on the bottom of a tiger's feet are soft and tender. Nor is the tiger's search for prey made easier by the alarm calls of the birds, deer, and monkeys that spot the hunter.

Although certain tigers do position themselves above game trails to ambush prey, they never expose themselves as the one depicted in this old print is doing.

To overcome these handicaps, *tigris* has developed special techniques. When Siberian tigers hunt bears and other prey, they lie on rock outcroppings above game trails and leap down on any that pass. As a matter of fact, cunning and stealth play an important part in the hunting methods of all the subspecies. Some tigers ambush their prey by hiding in vegetation. Others conceal themselves near water holes and spring on drinking animals. Still others stalk their prey.

Stalking is done mainly at night, when tigers roam slowly over their home range, usually following a regular beat. Once a potential victim is seen, the hunter moves very slowly and quietly. However, *tigris* does not head directly toward its target. It takes the route that offers the most cover, as its brown-striped markings and yellowish coat do not always blend into surrounding vegetation. But tigers have the ability to take advantage of even a little cover. One

When stalking prey, tigers lower the body and move slowly and quietly along the route that provides the most cover.

When close to the intended victim, the tiger charges.

observer reports that he saw a tiger successfully stalk a deer feeding in a field where the grass was only six inches high!

When as close to the prey as it can get without being detected, *tigris* charges. If fast enough, the hunter seizes its prize with the claws of its forefeet and its teeth. At the same time, the captive is thrown to the ground and, while falling, receives a vicious bite on some part of the neck.

For years hunters argued about the spot where tigers bit their prey. Some claimed *tigris* killed with a bite to the throat; others insisted it was the nape of the neck that was bitten. Modern research has established that, while both methods are used, the throat bite, which suffocates the prey, is more common. However, no matter which bite is employed, the tiger always makes sure it is not in a position to be stabbed with a horn or slashed with a hoof.

Diet

A proverb common in southern India maintains "If a tiger is hungry, it will eat grass." There is much truth to this ancient saying. Although carnivores, tigers do not feed solely on meat. When hungry, *tigris* will make a meal of berries, corn, grass, sugar cane, or anything edible it can find. However, its favorite dish is the flesh of antelope, deer, domestic stock, gaur, wapiti, wild boar, and young elephants or rhinos. *Tigris* also preys on both wild and domesticated water buffalo.

While many of these animals are found throughout *tigris'* range, others are native only to certain areas. Thus tigers in India prey on various species of deer, tigers in the Soviet Far East and in northern China feed on the Siberian wapiti, and tigers in central Asia dine on wild boar.

When large prey is lacking, *tigris* satisfies its ravenous appetite with crabs, fish, frogs, lizards, locusts, monkeys, snakes, termites, turtles, and rats and other rodents. Birds are also eaten but are not an important dish on the tiger's menu, although the Indian tiger considers peafowl a tasty snack. For its snack, the Indo-Chinese tiger chooses the prickly fruit of the durian tree. This is most unusual, as felids tend to avoid fruit covered with spines.

Zoologists are convinced that the solitary lifestyle of *tigris* developed because it is frequently forced to make a meal out of small creatures that are difficult to capture. Group hunting of such small prey would not only be a tremendous waste of time and energy but also would not provide enough food to satisfy all the hunters.

Tigers that kill large animals either drag or carry them to a secluded spot near the water. Staying close to the carcasses to protect them from poaching crows, hyenas, jackals, mongooses, and vultures, the tiger rests, eating whenever hungry, day or night. By the time *tigris* is finished with a deer, nothing is left save a few bones, a little skin, a hoof or two,

To dine undisturbed, tigers drag their prey to a secluded spot where they will not have to drive away vultures and other scavengers.

antlers, and certain internal organs that tigers find distasteful.

A good-sized deer furnishes food for several days. One Indian tiger—this subspecies can consume between forty and ninety pounds of meat during a single meal—was observed feeding on the carcass of a large buffalo for a week. Within two days the buffalo's flesh was putrid, but this made no difference to the tiger. *Tigris* relishes carrion.

Instead of staying near a kill until it has been completely eaten, a tiger may tote its victim a considerable distance, feed, and then place vegetation over the carcass to hide it from scavengers. All too often this is a waste of time.

Undoubtedly the most unusual item on the tiger's menu is

Bengal tiger carrying a chital fawn was photographed from an elephant's back in Kanha National Park, India.

porcupine flesh. Killing any species of Asian porcupine is a dangerous undertaking. When threatened, these spiky animals first sound a warning by shaking and rattling their tails. If the attacker does not retreat, the porcupine attacks, running rapidly backward with its barbed quills, some over a foot long, stiffly erect. While many tigers have never learned how to stop this furious charge without having dozens of quills embedded in their paws, neck, and mouth, others manage to kill porcupines with little damage to themselves. If quills can be pulled out easily, they are merely a nuisance. But often they prove impossible to remove, and soon the punctured area becomes infected. Gradually, the tiger grows too weak to stalk and capture prey. Suffering from pain and the pangs of hunger, *tigris* seeks easily acquired meat and begins to kill livestock. This, in turn, brings the once mighty predator into close contact with an animal it has little trouble killing—man.

Territorialism

A tiger's territory is that part of the home range containing the more or less permanent lairs in which the animal feels safe. Here, too, there is plenty of cover and an ample supply of food and water.

The size of the local tiger population or the lack of suitable habitat often makes it difficult for young tigers to establish territories of their own. Because such private preserves are in great demand, those already occupied are closely watched by range-seeking tigers. As soon as one is vacated, it is immediately claimed.

By maintaining relatively large territories that overlap those of two or more females, males ensure that they will find mates. Occupation of a tract where game is plentiful enables a tigress with young to secure food for herself and her ever hungry cubs without leaving them for long periods.

While sex is a factor in determining the size of a territory, a tiger's age, type of habitat, and the availability of prey are also important. Thus there is a wide variation in the extent of the various territories. For example, one field study established that an Indian tigress successfully raised a single cub in a six-mile square, while another investigation revealed that a female Siberian tiger living in an area where game was scarce had to hunt over 1600 square miles in order to survive.

Irrespective of size, territories with "No Trespassing Signs" posted at their boundaries are constantly patrolled by the residents. These signs, as noted, consist of a secretion from the anal glands mixed with urine and sprayed on trees, bushes, rocks, and other objects. Limits of territories are also defined by conspicuous piles of feces left in the middle of natural pathways, as well as by "scrapes." Tigers create scrapes by using the hind legs alternately to dig out two parallel indentations, approximately a foot and a half long, in the ground. The scrapes are them impregnated with scent.

By sniffing the musty odor that arises from the marks left by the owner of a territory, a transient tiger is able not only to determine the resident's age and sex but also to learn, if the scent is strong and fresh, that it may be dangerous to proceed. On the other hand, a faint scent indicates that the resident tiger has not been in the vicinity recently.

While all tigers engage in scent-marking, a few individuals have the habit of placing other warnings on the fringes of their territories. These tigers "blaze" trees. Standing on their hind legs, they reach up as high as possible, then rapidly rake their claws downward, cutting deep grooves in the trunk. In the process, they clean and sharpen their claws.

Relationships

Despite the fact that tigers are territorial, the ancient Chinese proverb "One hill cannot shelter two tigers" is not

Tigress photographed from a jeep in Ranthambhore National Park, India, leaves its "mark."

Tigers occasionally form a union, but such associations tend not to be long lasting.

true. As zoologist George Schaller points out, "Although the cat is essentially solitary, it is not unsociable."

Proof of the truth of Schaller's statement is furnished by the confirmed report of a hunting partnership formed by a leopard and a tiger, animals that normally shun one another. There are also accounts of immature tigers banding together and of as many as nine mature individuals of both sexes forming a union. However, field studies have determined that, as a general rule, associations among tigers are not long lasting.

Although a tiger may not have physical contact with its neighbors except during courtship, it is, as we have seen, aware of their movements and also recognizes them by sight and smell. While patrolling its territory, a tiger, as noted, also keeps in indirect communication with nearby resident tigers by marking and roaring.

Close relationships between tigers depend upon the animals' temperaments and moods. Some tigers are always tolerant of the transients that enter their territories. Others sometimes evict such trespassers; still others always do. In any case, the chances of an intruder's being ignored or welcomed are greatly increased if it is not of the same sex as the resident tiger. Males are apt to extend a friendly greeting to females. A male may rub his cheek against a tigress' cheek, neck, and head and express his pleasure at meeting her by raising his tail high as he rubs one of his flanks along her body.

Females may or may not accept a male's advances but they generally drive away trespassers of their own sex. Yet tigresses whose territories overlap may share a common area without engaging in aggressive encounters. This is because each female visits the area at different times. Incidentally, despite popular belief, male tigers do not wander about seeking fights with other males. Indeed, it appears that *tigris* instinctively seeks to avoid conflicts in which it might be so seriously injured that it would be unable to stalk and capture prey.

Instead of fighting, some neighboring tigers may hunt together. During meals, these partners display excellent "manners." Usually, the first tiger to eat is the one that made the kill, even if its companion is older and stronger. But many times, priority at a carcass is determined by size and strength.

However, despite the taking over of kills by dominant tigers, naturalists report many instances of carcasses being shared. There are even accounts of males, which are apt to kill cubs on sight, keeping their distance from a kill while a female and her young were eating. It has also been established that a female with one cub will wait patiently until a tigress with several offspring leaves a kill.

While waiting its turn to dine, a tiger stays about ten feet away from a kill so as not to intrude upon the feasting tiger. *Tigris* is jealous of its personal space and, as a general rule, keeps other tigers at a distance, except during courtship. But the pangs of hunger may drive two tigers to eat together. If their prey is a large animal, there is no problem. Each feeds on a different side of the carcass. If the prey is small, the tigers come in contact and hiss and growl constantly to indicate that their privacy is being invaded.

Tigers may socialize at kills and form temporary alliances, but fights between individuals do occur. These contests may be over the ownership of a kill, among residents and transients seeking territories, or between two vigorous males attracted to the same female.

But even when filled with jealous rage, rivals strive to avoid combat by using intimidation. First, they give warning that they are in an aggressive mood by twisting their ears so that the white markings on the backs are displayed. At the same time, the animals "make faces" at one another, employing various expressions such as fanning their whiskers, baring their teeth, and staring into each other's eyes to inform other tigers that they are feeling hostile. If one of the tigers looks away, both accept this as a sign of surrender and the contest ends without blood being shed.

However, if neither tiger lowers its gaze, the two emit coughing growls and start to paw at one another with their forelegs. The claws are sheathed until the first blow lands, then they are extended as the combatants stand on their hind legs and slash furiously while horrible noises come out of their open mouths. The battle may end suddenly when one of the tigers turns and flees, or it may continue for hours.

Occasionally a fight ends in death. But while such incidents are rare, serious injuries are not uncommon. Undoubtedly, more tigers would be mortally wounded or crippled for life if many fights did not come to an abrupt stop when one of the antagonists "surrendered" by rolling onto his back and holding all four legs upright. After acknowledging this sign of submission, many a victorious tiger has turned to claim the tigress that caused the fight, only to find that she has gone off with another male!

This Siberian tigress is showing the white spots on her ears, indicating that something is disturbing her. Perhaps she feels the photographer poses a threat to her cubs.

Courtship

Most animals have a short mating season. While this is true of the Siberian tiger, which mates in December, subspecies native to the tropics pair throughout the year. However, mating in these hot regions peaks between fall and early spring.

Females whose territories adjoin those of males are apt to welcome wooing by one of their neighbors. This is because the animals are likely to know each other and, in all probability, have mated in previous years. While males often have little difficulty in finding transient females that are seeking mates, they may have to battle rivals for the right to begin courtship. No fights between tigers are more vicious than those that occur when males clash over a tigress.

A tigress may, for one reason or another, rebuff a suitor. But some males that are not intimidated by a threatening expression, blazing eyes, bared teeth, and unsheathed claws frequently continue their wooing. In time, they may win the tigress' affection.

On the other hand, a rejected male may set off immediately in search of another female. He may not have far to go. An unattached female often accompanies a pair of tigers in the first stages of courtship and tries to induce the male to follow her. She sometimes succeeds. Males can be fickle. They have been known to court two females at the same time. Usually, however, once tigers pair up, they remain together. Their association may last for only a few days or the two may form a hunting partnership that lasts for several weeks.

Raising a Family

Male tigers have nothing to do with their cubs. Females assume all the work of caring for the young. A tigress' first task is to find a suitable nursery. Her choice may be a space between boulders, a tangle of fallen trees, a stand of tall grass, a thicket, or some other sheltered spot. Here, approximately fifteen weeks after mating, the cubs are born. While captive tigers often have large litters, the average litter in the wild consists of from one to three cubs.

Newborn tigers weigh about two pounds. Although fully striped, their coats are lighter in color than those of adults and the fur is thick and woolly. By the time the youngsters are five months old, this "baby hair" has been shed, but the ground color of young tigers' pelage is not identical to that of their parents until they are between two and three years old.

Not only are cubs helpless at birth but also their ears and eyes are closed. Both open within two weeks, but the babies are short-sighted for a while. This poses no problem, as the litter remains in the nursery zealously guarded by the tigress, who attends to their every need. The only time she leaves them is when she goes hunting.

Although cubs suckle until they are nine months old, the tigress brings them meat at a very early age. Their diet of milk and flesh causes the youngsters to gain weight quickly and they become stronger and more active. They engage in mock fights, chase one another, and play with the tigress' tail and ears. Affectionate mothers, female tigers tolerate their cubs' tugs and pawing. However tigresses are stern disciplinarians. Cubs that fail to respond promptly to calls ordering them to hide, scatter, or show themselves are apt to be lightly cuffed.

By the time the litter is two months old, it is following the tigress wherever she goes. During these excursions, the youngsters are taught to swim, avoid man, and stalk, attack, and kill prey. When six months old, the young tigers are

The Siberian tiger cub in the shadow of the shrubbery is better concealed from possible enemies than its sibling.

capable of helping their mother hunt but it is impossible for them to bring down a large animal—tigers do not get their sharp, strong, permanent teeth until they are a year old.

Gradually, the adolescents become more independent. Male cubs are more daring and often go off on their own for a day or two. While female cubs are not quite as adventurous, they, like their brothers, are in constant danger during this period.

Lacking experience, young tigers take unnecessary risks. As a result, many of them are injured or killed while hunting. But pointed horns, sharp hooves, and needle-like quills are not the first perils they have faced. Indeed, were it not for their mother, it is very likely that many cubs would be killed by a male tiger or eaten by a crocodile, jackal, hyena, leopard, or python. It is estimated that, in the face of predators, disease, accidents, and the activities of man, the survival rate of tiger cubs is less than fifty percent.

Undoubtedly, this figure would be considerably lower if immature tigers did not rely on their mother's protection and guidance until they are between eighteen months and two years of age. Eventually, however, they set out to find territories. Females that establish a home range and thrive will, if all goes well, seek mates when they become four years old and then raise families of their own.

5.
MAN AND TIGER

"It is well to look for whatever
we may lose."
—Pubillius Syrus

Man has persecuted the tiger for centuries. Nevertheless, *tigris* continued to thrive over much of its range until modern times. Today, the tiger is endangered. In less than a century, the world's population of free-roaming tigers has fallen dramatically. In 1900, wildlife experts estimated that some 440,000 Bengal tigers inhabited the jungles of India. The current tiger population of the subcontinent is presently set at 4000 individuals!

Meanwhile, with the possible exception of the Indo-Chinese tiger, which has a population of 1500 to 2000 animals, the state of the other subspecies is also critical. Field studies have shown that there are only about 100 Siberian tigers and between 500 and 800 Sumatran tigers. No one knows how many Chinese tigers there are. In recent years, this subspecies has rarely been seen in the wild.

Hopefully, the lack of sightings of *amoyensis* is due to its withdrawal into remote regions and not to ever diminishing numbers. As noted, the Bali tiger has vanished and the Caspian race is almost certainly extinct. It is also very likely that the Javan subspecies has disappeared or is on the verge of doing so.

Thus, even the most optimistic estimate of the world's wild tiger population ranges from 6000 to 7500 animals. After allowing for census errors, most wildlife experts agree that some 7000 tigers presently occupy what remains of the species' habitat.

What happened to the tiger? Less than one hundred years ago, villagers in much of India were forced to build high stockades around their homes to protect themselves and their livestock from marauding tigers. Nor were towns safe. To keep the great cats away, many towns were ringed with brightly burning fires every night. Despite these precautions,

Tigers can leap high in the air and are good climbers. These facts are the basis for this old print, showing two tigers attacking a tree house used as a shelter by tiger-hunt bearers.

hundreds of humans and thousands of buffalo, cattle, and goats were killed by tigers every year.

To encourage native hunters to destroy as many tigers as possible, several Indian states offered bounties. These campaigns, like others designed to eliminate a predator by paying its killers, failed. However, the bounty system did bring considerable wealth to certain hill tribes in Bengal. After killing a tiger, a tribesman would take its head to one official and collect the bounty, then present the animal's feet to another official and receive a second payment!

Relatively few tigers were killed by native hunters after 1858, when India came under British rule. The great majority were slain by English military and civil officers. These men not only reveled in the extremely dangerous sport of tiger hunting but also sincerely believed that tigers were vicious "vermin." Thus, in reporting their experiences in the jungle, these hunters filled their accounts with descriptions of the "malignant cunning" reflected in the eyes of *tigris*, "the cannibal hunger expressed in the curled lip," and the "glossy skin that is terrible to look at." When one Englishman reported bagging thirty-nine tigers in eleven days, he was highly praised. This was because public opinion held that the sooner the tiger was exterminated, the better.

However, there were a few individuals who did not approve of this wholesale slaughter. Among these were naturalists who vainly tried to defend *tigris* by pointing out that, were it not for the tiger's predation on deer and wild pigs, crop damage would be much greater than it was. But this obvious fact failed to impress those who considered tiger hunting to be not only a thrilling adventure but also a public service. There was far more concern that the unwritten laws governing tiger shooting, which were based on the British conception of "good sportsmanship," were followed. Typical of this code was the understanding that a

68

Most books written by author/hunters of yesteryear include a picture showing the daring sportsman bravely meeting the charge of a wounded and enraged tiger.

wounded tiger must be followed through the jungle until its suffering could be ended with a bullet.

Actually, rules had been established for tiger hunters long before the British took up the sport. The Mogul emperors of India who, as noted, permitted no one else to kill tigers, developed a ritualized pursuit of the great cat known as *shikar.* Armed only with bow and arrow, spear, or sword, the emperors slew tigers while mounted on fleet horses. Emperor Akbar was typical of these daring hunters. According to an ancient chronicler, Akbar once supervised fifty thousand men as they prepared for a hunt. When all was ready, trumpets blared and banners were raised as Akbar charged forward and "with one blow killed a tigress."

Not only were the Mogul emperors avid hunters but also

they were keen naturalists. None displayed more interest in wildlife than Jehangir, who kept detailed records of his observations. Jehangir probably would have encountered more birds and animals if his constant companion had not been a pet tiger!

The Moguls were not the only rulers who kept tigers. *Tigris* was wandering through European palaces at a very early date. Incidentally, the Greeks first saw a live tiger when Alexander the Great returned from India in 326 B.C. The Romans became familiar with the animal about two hundred years later.

Tigers fascinated several Roman emperors. Among them was Claudius, whose bedroom was guarded by four specially trained tigers. And the emperor Elagabalus not only rode through Rome in a chariot drawn by four tigers but also was accompanied by unleashed tigers that followed him like a pack of dogs whenever he strolled through his garden.

But no royal personage has ever been more attracted to *tigris* than Tipu Sultan (1753-1799), head of the Indian state of Mysore. Not only did Tipu's name mean tiger but also he maintained that he would rather live two days as a tiger than two hundred as a sheep. Tipu's obsession with *tigris* prompted him to adorn everything he owned, from handkerchiefs to throne, with the image of a tiger. Moreover, the great cat appeared on the uniforms and weapons of his soldiers, while his flag was inscribed "The Tiger Is God."

The most unusual items in Tipu's vast collection of objects glorifying the tiger were two life-sized mechanical dolls. One represented a red-coated British soldier, the other a tiger. When wound, the tiger would spring upon the soldier and go through the motions of devouring him!

As the years passed, the traditional *Shikar* was discarded. Native princes now hunted tigers with the rifles presented to

Since the days of ancient Rome, animal trainers have taught tigers to do various tricks. Indeed, many of the acts performed today by tigers in modern circuses were thrilling audiences over a thousand years ago.

71

them by representatives of British government. Good use was made of the gifts. In fact, the rifles enabled many a rajah to claim he had shot five hundred tigers. Meanwhile, hunters were also killing hundreds of tigers in hopes of bagging a record-setting trophy. There followed a reduction in the tiger population that was evident to native ruler and British sportsman alike. This led to tiger shootings being forbidden in certain areas and to closed seasons in others. The last move was most effective in states under nominal native rule, as the rajahs "took an extremely narrow view of poaching."

Although the Indian Forest Administration reported in the 1930's that the tiger's numbers were increasing, there was ample evidence this was only temporary. Too much of the tiger's habitat was being transformed into farmland to guarantee the species' survival. In fact, as early as 1877, author/hunter Captain Arthur Mundy warned, "In these modern times...the spread of civilization and the zeal of sportsmen have almost exterminated this breed of animal."

It was the gun, not the loss of habitat, that decimated the tiger population from 1930 to 1960. During these three decades, the royal owners of private hunting preserves and their guests, who included dignitaries from all parts of the world, slew thousands of tigers. While not as colorful as the hunts of the Mogul emperors, these "shoots" were quite spectacular:

> A whole village of tents would house the potentate, his guests, and innumerable servants in the middle of the jungle. Poised on bejeweled elephants, the hunters would take up positions along the path the tiger was expected to use to flee, while legions of beaters on foot would hem in the forest. Poised

There is more imagination than fact in this early print. It is extremely unlikely that five tigers would be seen together in such open country. Unlikely too is the hunter on the cliff.

high on his pachyderm, the hunter would be out of the tiger's reach. Moreover, the tiger, accustomed to seeing elephants which it occasionally passed in the forest, would approach without distrust. All there remained to do was shoot.

Another popular method of bagging a tiger was to make oneself comfortable on a platform built in a tree and wait for the prey to come and feed on a tied-up buffalo or goat. Shooting tigers from trees or an elephant's back was not nearly as dangerous as tracking *tigris* through the jungle. However, from time to time, a hunter was pulled out of a tree by an enraged tiger or tossed off the back of a frightened elephant stampeding to safety.

Tiger-shooting at night from a platform. Note the tethered goats used to "bait" tigris. Today, scientists bait tigers in order to tranquilize them and examine them in safety.

Meanwhile, habitat destruction and uncontrolled hunting were also threatening the survival of the other subspecies of tiger. Conservationists, realizing that they had neither the money nor the manpower to ensure the future of all the subspecies, decided to devote their efforts to saving the Indian tiger. The first step was taken in 1969, when the International Union for the Conservation of Nature and Natural Resources met in New Delhi. The Union entered *Panthera tigris tigris* in the *Red Data Book*, which lists endangered species. The following year, Prime Minister Indira Gandhi sponsored legislation that not only banned tiger hunting in India but also made the sale of tiger skins illegal. To aid India in stamping out an active black market in tiger pelts, most countries barred their importation.

74

Inspired by India's action, other Asian nations with populations of tigers provided official protection. Before long, all the subspecies were recorded in the *Red Data Book*. At the same time, fearing that the only living tigers would be in zoos within a few years, scientists began to collect all available data about captive tigers. Undoubtedly, had such information been available earlier, both the Caspian and Javan tigers might have been saved from extinction. No specimen of the vanished Bali tiger was ever kept in captivity so far as is known.

While zoologists on the staff of the Leipzig Zoo in Germany who specialize in the Felidae strive to keep up-to-date records of tigers in zoos, other authorities seek to insure the survival of *tigris* in the wild. For example, the World

It is up to the human race to make sure that the tiger always has a place to hide in the wild.

Wildlife Fund and the governments of Bangladesh, Bhutan, India, and Nepal are united in Project Tiger. The aim of this international effort is to set aside reserves where *tigris*, guarded from poachers, can roam freely.

Over the years, Project Tiger has accomplished a great deal. However, even this project's most enthusiastic supporters realize that the tiger can never regain its former numbers. Man has taken over too much of its native habitat. Indeed, some wildlife experts are convinced that, despite Project Tiger, the future of *tigris* is bleak. These individuals base their contention on the belief that scattered sanctuaries of limited acreage cannot support enough unrelated tigers of breeding age to guarantee the species' survival in the wild.

One thing is certain. The future of *tigris* depends upon man. Hopefully, we humans will never forget that the tiger, like all of God's creations, has its place on Earth.

INDEX